MARLBOROUGH
in old photographs

Crown court. A terrace off Kingsbury Street. Photographed in the 1930's shortly before its demolition. An example of working class housing typical of the many courts and terraces behind the street line. Much of this type of housing was cleared when new houses became available on the perimeter of the town from 1920 onwards.

MARLBOROUGH
in old photographs

collected by

Michael Gray
Francis James

ALAN SUTTON

Alan Sutton Publishing Limited
17a Brunswick Road
Gloucester

First published 1982

Copyright © 1982 Michael Gray and Francis James

All rights reserved. No part of this publication may be
reproduced, stored in a retrieval system, or transmitted,
in any form or by any means, electronic, mechanical photocopying,
recording or otherwise, without the prior permission of
the publishers and copyright holder.

British Library Cataloguing in Publication Data

Gray, Michael
   Marlborough in old photographs.
   1. Marlborough (Wiltshire)—History—Pictorial
   works
   I. Title   II. James, Francis
   942.3'17   DA690.M46

   ISBN 0-86299-018-1

Typesetting and origination by
Alan Sutton Publishing Limited.
Photoset Baskerville 10/11
Printed in Great Britain
by Page Bros (Norwich) Limited

Acknowledgements

The authors wish to offer their most sincere thanks to all those who offered their treasured photographs, and who thereby made this book possible. They hope that this small collection of old photographs, culled from a wealth of possibilities, will give them pleasure and satisfaction for many years to come.

Particular thanks are offered to: R.J. Ashley, Jess Chandler, Wally Clarke, Bob Cooke, James Edwards, Peter Free, Mrs Greenaway, G. Kempson, P. Hamilton Leggett, Mrs Lane, A.B. Loncraine, The Mowat Collection, Dr. Tim Maurice, The Ken Nunn Collection, Frank Odey, Mrs Pettie, Real Photograph Company, Dennis White, Wiltshire Newspapers Ltd., James Young.

The copying of the original photographs has been undertaken by Martin J. Robinson MPA of Larkhall Studios, Bath, and Mrs. Alma Shaw of Oare. Owing to the poor condition of many of the originals this has been a task of considerable difficulty which they have discharged admirably.

About the Authors

Michael Gray was educated at Marlborough Grammar School, and has lived all his life in Marlborough. His family have roots in the town more than a century long. For many years, an antique dealer of distinction, he has been actively campaigning for the conservation of the town's fabric, and his personal collection of photographs spawned the idea to invite others to collaborate in producing this volume.

Francis James collaborated!

Introduction

As a visual record of the life of town and village, old photographs take over where painting, engraving and lithograph leave off. Whereas the painter and engraver, in the main, looked for the picturesque view, and the important building, the photographer pointed his camera at whatever caught his attention. The sublime event, the ridiculous detail are all caught on the film. The photographer also penetrated the quiet and secret places of the town, and often unconsciously recorded many of the more intimate details of life in those earlier times. It is this intimacy which makes old photographs so fascinating. The authors hope they may be forgiven for including a number of photographs which are rather indistinct. It was felt that the picture of Marlborough since 1860 would have been the poorer for their omission.

Architecturally, it is said that all the buildings look more satisfying in the old photographs than they do today. Where they remain the same, we breathe a sigh of relief; where they are altered, it is usually for the worse. In some cases, where we look at a view taken in 1880, we are seeing buildings which could have been photographed identically in 1780 or even 1680. In other cases the changes have been subtly wrought by a combination of long local ownership, and the skill and advice of Marlborough builders. The ground floor elevations of today's national chain stores qualify in neither respect, and the result is all to plain to be seen. The defence that the costs of sensitive restoration are prohibitive, is inadmissable, for it has been achieved locally by those who really care. Despite the stringency of our planning system, which did not exist when 18th and 19th century alterations were made, we have lost more since its inception, than in the whole of the last two centuries. Even ealy penticed buildings, which are the town's most famous feature have been removed and replaced without sympathy.

In the present century, change has swept through all aspects of life at an ever growing pace, sweeping away indiscriminately much of the good and bad alike. Marlborough has fortunately dragged its feet, and has thereby avoided the wholesale destruction which became a commonplace sight in the 1950s and 60s.

If this book has a value, it is to act as a check list of what we possessed, to be compared with what we have now, and to prevent future destruction of our tangible cultural heritage. If we do not prevent this destruction as it is in our power to do, then future publications will carry the rebuke from generation to generation.

Introduction

Above July 1864 – Celebrations surrounding the completion of the "Royal Wiltshire" Lifeboat, funds for which had been collected locally. A rare picture of the old Town Hall, built in 1793, demolished 1900.
Below Earliest known view of High Street, taken about 1864.

Above 3 views of 1793 Town Hall, as refronted in Bath stone in 1885. This building was replaced by the present Town Hall in 1901 because it was said to be inadequate for the Quarter Sessions. Ironically they are no longer held here. The 1653 date plaque on the north side refers to the construction date of the earliest Town Hall.

Below High Street c. 1890. The Horse Bus belonged to the Castle and Ball Hotel for transporting passengers to the station.

C.H. Leader, the proprietor of the Castle and Ball Hotel, standing beside the hitching rails outside the building in 1907. He is speaking to his son, who as Capt. Leader followed a distinguished military career.

One of the few early photographs of the market, taken in May 1892. At that time the open space beneath the Town Hall formed a covered site for part of the market.

The present Town Hall, shown soon after its completion on the occasion of the distribution of mugs following Edward VII's coronation in 1902.

Above The Fire Brigade deliver the puddings to the street banquet, which probably celebrated the 1902 coronation. Notice the marquee erected in the High Street, a proposition which would meet stiff official resistance from today's authorities!
Below West end of High Street, showing St Peter's church, c. 1905. Lack of traffic conveys an enviable sense of peace.

Nos. 33 and 34 High Street, the shop of Stephen Neate, erected after the great fire of 1653, decorated for the visit of the Duke of Albany in 1882. The following pictures illustrate some of his advertising material and the fire which tragically destroyed these buildings in 1976.

PLEASE ADDRESS ALL LETTERS AND GOODS IN FULL.   Telegrams: STEPHEN NEATE.

STEPHEN H. NEATE
FURNISHING WAREHOUSEMAN
Undertaker

INTEREST CHARGED ON
OVERDUE ACCOUNTS,
WHICH ARE DUE ON
DELIVERY.

AGENT FOR THE PHOENIX
ASSURANCE COMPANY—
FIRE, LIFE, BURGLARY
AND ALL PURPOSES.

LICENSED VALUER.
Carpets. Window Blinds.
Casement Curtains.
Furniture Draperies
of all kinds.

Restorations. Repairs.
Paper Hangings.
Picture Frame Maker.

FUNERALS DIRECTED
& FURNISHED.

34, HIGH STREET,
MARLBOROUGH.

192

ESTABLISHED 46 YEARS.

Please address all Letters
STEPHEN H. NEATE, 34, High Street, MARLBOROUGH.

Undertaker, Valuer, and Complete House Furnisher.

HOUSEHOLD REMOVALS, WITH GREATEST DISPATCH, BY ROAD OR RAIL.
SEE NUMEROUS TESTIMONIALS.

WINDOW BLINDS. CARPETS. DRAPERIES. RECOVERINGS AND REPAIRS
ANTIQUE FURNITURE DEALER.

Marlborough Mop Fairs are held on the Saturdays before and after Old Michaelmas Day, and are still held in the High Street despite strong official pressure to move them elsewhere. This Victorian view shows the high standard of fair ground art at this period.

Above The Fair c. 1905. Note very up-to-date roundabout with new fangled motor cars.
Below & Opposite The Fair in the 1920's. Jennings "Wonderful Whales" was still in use into the 1950's. Note the 1d fare for the gallopers.

Alderman Thomas Free at the Town Pump in 1912. He was a member of a prominent local family who started a furniture and cabinet making business in the town which still flourishes today. He was mayor in 1901, 1910, 1911, 1923, and 1924. The trough and pump stood towards the south side of the High Street and were removed to facilitate the flow of traffic in 1929.

Jesse Dubber, a local rag and bone man, was a familiar sight with his donkey and cart, for many years. He appears in an oil painting of the 1840's. This photograph was taken in Russell Square about 1870.

Four views of the Marlborough Rifle Volunteers, taken on Shrove Tuesday 1876. Horse drawn personnel carrier in Riding School Yard. Across the yard was the Corn Exchange, which doubled as their depot. Weapons were stored in vaults beneath.

Assembled company, from the left:
Mortimer, Stanley, Leadley, Dale, Smith, Foster, Capt. Price, Andrews, Sgt. Turner, Hawkins, Cane, Gwillim, Bond, Sgt. Pocock.

Mock arrest.

Sgts. Pocock and Turner. The rifles are Sniders, used in the regular army 1864–1871.

A member of the Maurice family in the uniform of the Royal Wiltshire Yeomanry about the turn of the century. This was the service yeomanry regiment formed in 1799.

Above Parade of the Motor Corps in 1903, drawn up for inspection by Lt. Roberts. Presumably collected together to provide the transport for foreign military observers at the manoeuvres on Salisbury Plain.
Below & Following The Castle and Ball was taken over by the government for the accommodation of foreign observers from France, Germany, Italy, Japan, Portugal, Spain and U.S.A. The English driver is Major Fasson and the German delegation comprised Majors Count von de Groeben, von der Schulenberg and Capt. von Poseck.

During the Great War, the High Street was frequently used as a park for transport units.

Below A detachment of colonial artillery, parked outside the Corn Exchange during the war of 1914–18.

A collection of cartes de visite of several Marlborough photographers. It is to these and their colleagues that the authors are indebted, for much of the material in the book.

This building, 13 New Road, was a purpose built butchers shop and slaughterhouse, constructed in 1800. It served as such until 1977. These two views are of the shop dressed overall for Christmas under two successive ownerships just before and after the Great War.

The Sunday promenade in the 1890's, a Marlborough custom, more redolent of Continental practice.

Nos. 99–102 High Street, c. 1880. The building on the left, Pope's Ironworks, is the oldest secular building in Marlborough, dating from c. 1500, but refronted after 1653. The Georgian Terraced front dates from c. 1740. The dignified variety of the ground floor elevations, shown in so many of these pictures, is in sharp contrast to the blatant commercialism of today.

Mr. Phillips the Ironmonger outside his shop at 141 High Street in 1900. The Midland Bank now stands on this site.

Nos. 17–21 High Street in the 1870's. The Printing Office, also the Post Office, was destroyed by a disastrous fire on April 13th, 1879. The fire was spotted by a constable at about 1.30 a.m. on Easter morning. The Marlborough engine was delayed, owing to uncertainty about who had the keys. When it appeared the hoses leaked badly and shortly afterwards burst. A bucket chain was formed to the town pump and horsemen sent to Swindon, Pewsey and Savernake to summon more engines. The Savernake crew was delayed because the horses pulling the cartload of men bolted with the shafts, leaving some embarrassment behind. Even the powerful Swindon engine, arriving at 7 a.m. failed to prevent the total destruction of the Post Office, and the building next door (out of the picture), subsequently collapsed. A new fire engine was, as a result, ordered for the Marlborough brigade.

Above Marlborough Fire Brigade and the "new engine" at a farm in the 1890's.
Below The first motorised appliance, a Merryweather, delivered in 1926, at a practice at Marlborough College. This machine remained in use up to 1939, when it was sent for war duty in London.

Alma Place 1916. Notice the outside sinks. No indoor plumbing until 1922. Mrs Pettie, on the extreme left, still lives there.

Bernard Court c. 1930 (rear of 75 High Street). What did the mysterious carved head represent?

Chivers, jewellers and watch makers, 11 High Street. Mr. T. Baker and his father are standing in the doorway. The car is a 1930 Standard 9.

Above The complete workforce of Messrs. T.E. Leadley, builders, outside no. 96 High Street, about 1924. The horsedrawn transport has been pushed to one side to give prominence to the 'T' Ford lorries.
Below The Smith family of Moffat House, 10 London Road, drapers, pictured about 1924 with their motor cars; a a Morris Cowley and a Daimler.

A locomotive accident at Marlborough engine shed, during the great snowstorm of January 1881.

Above Marlborough Low Level station in its heyday between the wars.
Below 0-6-0 locomotive 1007 up passenger train at Marlborogh 1931.

Above 4-4-4 tank engine No 18 hauling the 2.35pm Swindon/Andover train entering Marlborough 17th April 1914.
Below 2-6-0 locomotive No 16 with the 6.43am Cheltenham/Andover goods leaving Marlborough 17th April 1914.

Marlborough High Level station August 1927.

Marlborough High Level station shortly before demolition 1964

Above The Great Western Railway operated a bus service from 1904
Below onwards, from Marlborough Station to Calne, via Avebury.

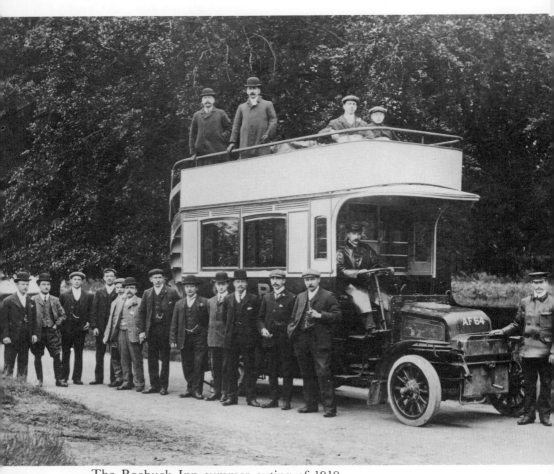
The Roebuck Inn summer outing of 1910.

A Marlborough outing to Salisbury on Duck's charabanc.

Oare village outing to Marlborough in 1905. Notice the water driven fire bell above William Free's warehouse. The fire engine lived beneath the arches.

Above The first aeroplane to land in the borough, a Bleriot monoplane.
Below The aeronaut, M. Selmet, competing in the Daily Mail aeroplane race of 1912, alighted at Marlborough, where he dined at the Ailesbury Arms with the mayor, Ald. T. Free, who is pictured sitting in the machine. M. Selmet stands to the right wearing goggles. After refuelling with petrol, supplied by Bell's garage, M. Selmet continued to Bath.

RUS IN URBE
Barton Farm, whilst strictly outside the borough, was yet close enough to form part of the town's life. These photographs came from the family album of the Edwards family, who occupied the farm for many years.

Thrashing operations in the 1920's.

Above Interior of the C17th Great South Barn, showing the Penny and Porter corn grading machine. This barn was totally destroyed by fire in 1976.
Below Albert Scott holding the shorthorn bull.

Fred Eyles and Walter Scott the foreman driving the farm's first two tractors. Fred Eyles is driving an International 10/20 of 1920.

Shepherd Payne, and **over**, shepherds Payne and Holmes. Mr. Payne came to see Mr. Edwards four days before lambing to tell him he himself would never see the lambing begin. He said he had fallen on the downs and seen the angels calling him. Two days later he died and was buried in Preshute churchyard, with the traditional hank of wool in his coffin.

Above The Edwards family pony trap containing the children and their Nanny, May Fiddler.
Below The family Model 'T' Ford of about 1920.

The old Grammar School, built in 1791 – demolished in 1904, when it was replaced by the present building.

The opening of the Grammar School Rifle Range by Sir Ian Hamilton in 1907 at the invitation of Dr. J.B. Maurice, who stands top hatted to the left of the dais. In front of him stands his son, Dr. W.B. Maurice.

Above A view of London Road in Edwardian days. Five Alls Inn on the right. All the buildings on the left hand side of the street have been destroyed.

Below The Parade c. 1905. The sense of enclosure has been lost by the demolition of the buildings facing the camera.

Above The Borough Arms, 15 The Parade, landlord George White. It was closed in 1913, when there were 25 licensed premises in the borough, giving a ratio of one licensed house to every 176 inhabitants.
Below The George Inn, from which George Lane takes its name. A fine jetted building of about 1600, demolished in 1947. The Catholic church now stands on the site. Probably a drovers pub, providing ample grazing.

The Town Mill before the upper floors were destroyed in the 1950's. This was in full operation until 1926.

Above A late Victorian view of the Green showing Eagle House, which was rebuilt in 1906. The building on the right was the White Hart Inn, which ceased to hold a license in 1913.

Below West view of The Green showing the large trees outside No. 1. These were felled in the 1930's.

East view of the Green, c. 1930, is little changed from today.

A runaway bus embedded in Eggleton's shop about 1935. This building was, strangely, later demolished by a lorry, and rebuilt as the National Provincial Bank.

This fine set of pictures was taken by the Reverend Lane just before the last war, when the wheelwrights craft was still practised. Arthur Potter's workshop still survives in Russell Square, and is a purpose built wheelwright's shop built in 1831. He produced his last new farm cart in about 1947 for Mr. Wroth of Clatford.

Above Mr. Potter is shown with his assistant Harry Werrell operating the tyre bender. By winding the handle the iron tyre bar was bent into a circle. The ends were then ready for 'shutting' or welding together.

Below The iron tyre has been placed on the ground and is being heated in a circular fire. Wood shavings are being thrown onto the blaze. The up-to-date wheelwright used a special furnace for this operation.

Above The wheel has been screwed down on to the tyring platform, a circular iron plate an inch and a quarter thick with a hole in the centre to admit the wheel hub. Mr. Potter armed with two 'tyring dogs' is holding the hot tyre while his assistant locates it on the wheel with the aid of a sledgehammer.

Below Now in place the tyre is being quenched with cans of water. As it cooled the tyre contracted tightly onto the wheel. A series of sharp clicks announced that the spokes were going home into the mortices, and the dowels into their dowel holes. This tightening also increased the 'dish' of the wheel. As the centre screw was loosened the stock rose up an inch or more.

Whilst tyring was the modern method of finsihing the wheel (dating from the 1880's) the older method was shoeing. Here a series of iron 'strakes' each joined two sections or 'felloes' of the rim. It was less strong and more expensive than tyring, but surprisingly it was still a method being used by Mr. Potter. In this picture Mr. Potter is hammering a 'strake' into position. Mr. Werrell is gripping the other end to hold it in position. The tool which is clamping the 'felloes' togehter is called a 'samson'.

The 'samson' and sledge hammer. The nuts were screwed up to clamp the 'felloes' together.

Celebrations of Edward VII's coronation in 1902. Staff, patrons and family of The Jolly Butcher, Lavingtons the auctioneers and The Marlborough Times feast on the pavement. Community spirit is evident in the window boxes and lavish street decorations.

An impressive array of cyclists drawn up before the Town Hall about 1890. Note the presence of early safety cycles as well as the obsolescent penny farthings. The C18th shop windows were shortly to disappear.

The opening of the new Post Office. Following the 1879 fire the Post Office moved to No. 131 High Street (Dewhursts) and moved again to the present site in 1910.

The Golden Jubilee of Queen Victoria was celebrated by an ox roast shown here together with Solicitor Gwillim's dinner ticket.

Jubilee Celebration,

June 21st.   1887.

DINNER TICKET.

:ach Person to bring Cup, Plate, Knife, and Fork.

For Number of Table see other side.

Edwardian Whist drive in the new Town Hall. Notice the fine original gasoliers.

George V's coronation was marked by this magnificent bonfire on the Common. Hat in hand stands the mayor, Ald. T. Free.

This is the only known view of the interior of the Corn Exchange. The occasion is a children's tea party celebrating a royal event — but which? Poverty does not seem to have prevented all the children being well turned out.

A common feature of the Marlborough scene was the town band, here shown playing for the newly elected mayor, Ald. T. Free in 1910, outside Hughenden House.

The town listens to a stirring performance by the band on the occasion of the Diamond Jubilee of Queen Victoria. Mr. Bambridge, the College organist, conducts from the Town Hall steps.

Marlborough Town Silver Band, 1906.

St. Peter's from Treacle Bolly, showing The Waimate the Georgian house on the right. W.S. Bambridge lived here from 1864. As well as being organist to the College for many years he was a noted local sportsman and chairman of most local clubs.

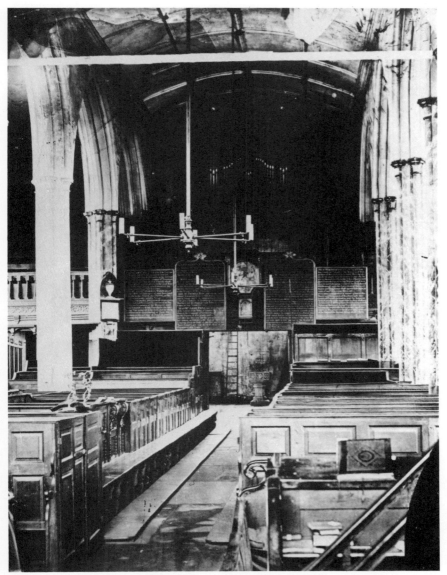
St. Peter's church before Wyatt's 'restoration' of 1862.

The box pews date from around 1700. Notice the servants' benches outside the central aisle. The Western Gallery dates from 1625 and the organ from 1820. The large mural clock dated 1746 now hangs in St. Mary's. The tie bar across the Chancel arch was found to be all that prevented collapse. All these features were lost in 1862 including the gracious five light window.

Though a faded picture this is the first photograph of St. Peter's after the restoration and clearly shows the new masonry round the east window.

St. Peter's church fete July 8th, 1903, opened by Lady Marjorie Bruce. The gardens of Lloran House and St. Peter's Rectory were combined for the occasion.

Inter parochial rivalry was also a feature of town life. Here the 1908 cricket teams prepare to do battle.

Above 1913 found Marlborough playing host to the national town criers competition. The mayor E.N. Colbran stands with his corporation and the contestants on the Town Hall steps.
Below Wiltshire Constabulary 'specials' in 1940.
unknown, unknown, Edge, Sharman, Wingrove, G. Kempton, A. Williams, Maples, unknown, D. Free, unknown
W. Neate, Sgt. Spreckley, Sgt. Gale, Supt. Gibson, Sp. Ins. A. Keller, Tom Bernard, unknown, McCrall
Burgess, unknown, unknown, Scattergood, Bill Dawes, Bob Smith, J. Fletcher, unkown

Above 1870's view of the College Court, showing part of the 1848 chapel on the right. Tuck is being dispensed by Mr. Duck from his barrow.
Below The Court 20 years later. The open air fives courts were shortly to disappear to make way for the library block.

An Edwardian Prize Day. Notice the trees (see page 91). New gates, chapel and porters lodge attest to the growing prosperity of the College.

The Reverend G.C. Bell, Master from 1876–1903, at the door of C House. Notice bowler hatted reporter on the right.

The College kitchens of 1902 pictured, still in use in the 1930's.

Manton Village. Victorian and Elizabethan views.